Book of 100 Storyboard Templates

Matthew M. Davis
DVGPro.com

Project Title:_____Production Co._____

Director:_____ Page #_____

Scene:_____Shot #_____ Location:_____

```
┌─────────────────────────────────────────────────┐
│                                                 │
│                                                 │
│                                                 │
│                                                 │
│                                                 │
│                                                 │
│                                                 │
│                                                 │
│                                                 │
│                                                 │
└─────────────────────────────────────────────────┘
```

Still ☐ Pan ☐ Dolly ☐ Tilt ☐ Zoom ☐ Pedestal ☐ Truck ☐ Handheld ☐

Description of action: _____

_____

_____

_____

_____

_____

_____

_____

_____

_____

Other cues: _____

_____

_____

_____

_____

Equipment needed: _____

_____

_____

_____

Project Title:_____Production Co._____

Director:_____ Page #_____

Scene:_____Shot #_____ Location:_____

```
┌─────────────────────────────────────────────────────────┐
│                                                         │
│                                                         │
│                                                         │
│                                                         │
│                                                         │
│                                                         │
│                                                         │
│                                                         │
│                                                         │
│                                                         │
│                                                         │
│                                                         │
│                                                         │
└─────────────────────────────────────────────────────────┘
```

Still ☐ Pan ☐ Dolly ☐ Tilt ☐ Zoom ☐ Pedestal ☐ Truck ☐ Handheld ☐

Description of action: _____

_____

_____

_____

_____

_____

_____

_____

_____

_____

Other cues: _____

_____

_____

_____

_____

Equipment needed: _____

_____

_____

_____

Project Title:_____Production Co._____

Director:_____ Page #_____

Scene:_____Shot #_____ Location:_____

```
┌─────────────────────────────────────────────────────┐
│                                                     │
│                                                     │
│                                                     │
│                                                     │
│                                                     │
│                                                     │
│                                                     │
│                                                     │
│                                                     │
│                                                     │
│                                                     │
│                                                     │
│                                                     │
│                                                     │
│                                                     │
└─────────────────────────────────────────────────────┘
```

Still ☐ Pan ☐ Dolly ☐ Tilt ☐ Zoom ☐ Pedestal ☐ Truck ☐ Handheld ☐

Description of action: _____

_____

_____

_____

_____

_____

_____

_____

_____

Other cues: _____

_____

_____

_____

_____

Equipment needed: _____

_____

_____

_____

Project Title:_____Production Co._____

Director:_____ Page #_____

Scene:_____Shot #_____ Location:_____

Still ☐ Pan ☐ Dolly ☐ Tilt ☐ Zoom ☐ Pedestal ☐ Truck ☐ Handheld ☐

Description of action: _____

_____

_____

_____

_____

_____

_____

_____

_____

_____

Other cues: _____

_____

_____

_____

_____

Equipment needed: _____

_____

_____

_____

Project Title:_____Production Co._____

Director:_____ Page #_____

Scene:_____Shot #_____ Location:_____

Still ☐ Pan ☐ Dolly ☐ Tilt ☐ Zoom ☐ Pedestal ☐ Truck ☐ Handheld ☐

Description of action: _____

_____

_____

_____

_____

_____

_____

_____

_____

_____

Other cues: _____

_____

_____

_____

_____

Equipment needed: _____

_____

_____

_____

Project Title:_____Production Co._____

Director:_____ Page #_____

Scene:_____Shot #_____ Location:_____

```
┌─────────────────────────────────────────────────┐
│                                                 │
│                                                 │
│                                                 │
│                                                 │
│                                                 │
│                                                 │
│                                                 │
│                                                 │
│                                                 │
│                                                 │
│                                                 │
│                                                 │
└─────────────────────────────────────────────────┘
```

Still □ Pan □ Dolly □ Tilt □ Zoom □ Pedestal □ Truck □ Handheld □

Description of action: _____

_____

_____

_____

_____

_____

_____

_____

_____

Other cues: _____

_____

_____

_____

_____

Equipment needed: _____

_____

_____

_____

Project Title:_____Production Co._____
Director:_____ Page #_____
Scene:_____Shot #_____ Location:_____

Still ☐ Pan ☐ Dolly ☐ Tilt ☐ Zoom ☐ Pedestal ☐ Truck ☐ Handheld ☐

Description of action: _____
_____
_____
_____
_____
_____
_____
_____
_____
_____

Other cues: _____
_____
_____
_____
_____
_____

Equipment needed: _____
_____
_____
_____

Project Title:_____Production Co._____

Director:_____ Page #_____

Scene:_____Shot #_____ Location:_____

```
┌─────────────────────────────────────────────────────────┐
│                                                         │
│                                                         │
│                                                         │
│                                                         │
│                                                         │
│                                                         │
│                                                         │
│                                                         │
│                                                         │
│                                                         │
│                                                         │
│                                                         │
│                                                         │
│                                                         │
└─────────────────────────────────────────────────────────┘
```

Still ☐ Pan ☐ Dolly ☐ Tilt ☐ Zoom ☐ Pedestal ☐ Truck ☐ Handheld ☐

Description of action:_____

_____

_____

_____

_____

_____

_____

_____

_____

Other cues:_____

_____

_____

_____

_____

Equipment needed:_____

_____

_____

_____

Project Title:_____Production Co._____
Director:_____ Page #_____
Scene:_____Shot #_____ Location:_____

```
┌─────────────────────────────────────────────┐
│                                               │
│                                               │
│                                               │
│                                               │
│                                               │
│                                               │
│                                               │
│                                               │
│                                               │
│                                               │
│                                               │
│                                               │
└─────────────────────────────────────────────┘
```

Still ☐ Pan ☐ Dolly ☐ Tilt ☐ Zoom ☐ Pedestal ☐ Truck ☐ Handheld ☐

Description of action: _____
_____
_____
_____
_____
_____
_____
_____
_____
_____

Other cues: _____
_____
_____
_____
_____

Equipment needed: _____
_____
_____
_____

Project Title:_____Production Co._____
Director:_____ Page #_____
Scene:_____Shot #_____ Location:_____

Still ☐ Pan ☐ Dolly ☐ Tilt ☐ Zoom ☐ Pedestal ☐ Truck ☐ Handheld ☐

Description of action: _____
_____
_____
_____
_____
_____
_____
_____
_____

Other cues: _____
_____
_____
_____
_____

Equipment needed: _____
_____
_____
_____
_____

Project Title:_____Production Co._____
Director:_____ Page #_____
Scene:_____ Shot #_____ Location:_____

Still ☐ Pan ☐ Dolly ☐ Tilt ☐ Zoom ☐ Pedestal ☐ Truck ☐ Handheld ☐

Description of action: _____
_____
_____
_____
_____
_____
_____
_____
_____
_____

Other cues: _____
_____
_____
_____
_____

Equipment needed: _____
_____
_____
_____

Project Title:_____Production Co._____

Director:_____ Page #_____

Scene:_____Shot #_____ Location:_____

Still ☐ Pan ☐ Dolly ☐ Tilt ☐ Zoom ☐ Pedestal ☐ Truck ☐ Handheld ☐

Description of action: _____

_____

_____

_____

_____

_____

_____

_____

_____

Other cues: _____

_____

_____

_____

_____

Equipment needed: _____

_____

_____

_____

Project Title:_____Production Co._____
Director:_____ Page #_____
Scene:_____Shot #_____ Location:_____

```
┌─────────────────────────────────────────────────┐
│                                                 │
│                                                 │
│                                                 │
│                                                 │
│                                                 │
│                                                 │
│                                                 │
│                                                 │
│                                                 │
│                                                 │
└─────────────────────────────────────────────────┘
```

Still ☐ Pan ☐ Dolly ☐ Tilt ☐ Zoom ☐ Pedestal ☐ Truck ☐ Handheld ☐

Description of action: _____
_____
_____
_____
_____
_____
_____
_____
_____
_____
_____

Other cues: _____
_____
_____
_____
_____

Equipment needed: _____
_____
_____
_____

Project Title:_____Production Co._____

Director:_____ Page #_____

Scene:_____Shot #_____ Location:_____

Still ☐ Pan ☐ Dolly ☐ Tilt ☐ Zoom ☐ Pedestal ☐ Truck ☐ Handheld ☐

Description of action: _____
_____
_____
_____
_____
_____
_____
_____
_____
_____

Other cues: _____
_____
_____
_____
_____

Equipment needed: _____
_____
_____
_____

Project Title:_____Production Co._____

Director:_____ Page #_____

Scene:_____Shot #_____ Location:_____

Still ☐ Pan ☐ Dolly ☐ Tilt ☐ Zoom ☐ Pedestal ☐ Truck ☐ Handheld ☐

Description of action: _____

_____
_____
_____
_____
_____
_____
_____
_____
_____

Other cues: _____

_____
_____
_____
_____

Equipment needed: _____

_____
_____
_____

Project Title:_____ Production Co._____

Director:_____ Page #_____

Scene:_____Shot #_____ Location:_____

Still ☐ Pan ☐ Dolly ☐ Tilt ☐ Zoom ☐ Pedestal ☐ Truck ☐ Handheld ☐

Description of action: _____

_____

_____

_____

_____

_____

_____

_____

_____

_____

Other cues: _____

_____

_____

_____

_____

Equipment needed: _____

_____

_____

_____

Project Title:_____Production Co._____

Director:_____ Page #_____

Scene:_____Shot #_____ Location:_____

Still ☐ Pan ☐ Dolly ☐ Tilt ☐ Zoom ☐ Pedestal ☐ Truck ☐ Handheld ☐

Description of action: _____

_____

_____

_____

_____

_____

_____

_____

Other cues: _____

_____

_____

_____

_____

Equipment needed: _____

_____

_____

_____

Project Title:_____Production Co._____
Director:_____ Page #_____
Scene:_____Shot #_____ Location:_____

```
┌─────────────────────────────────────────────────┐
│                                                 │
│                                                 │
│                                                 │
│                                                 │
│                                                 │
│                                                 │
│                                                 │
│                                                 │
│                                                 │
│                                                 │
│                                                 │
│                                                 │
└─────────────────────────────────────────────────┘
```

Still ☐ Pan ☐ Dolly ☐ Tilt ☐ Zoom ☐ Pedestal ☐ Truck ☐ Handheld ☐

Description of action: _____
_____
_____
_____
_____
_____
_____
_____
_____
_____

Other cues: _____
_____
_____
_____
_____

Equipment needed: _____
_____
_____
_____

Project Title:_____Production Co._____
Director:_____Page #_____
Scene:_____Shot #_____Location:_____

```



```

Still ☐ Pan ☐ Dolly ☐ Tilt ☐ Zoom ☐ Pedestal ☐ Truck ☐ Handheld ☐

Description of action:_____
_____
_____
_____
_____
_____
_____
_____

Other cues:_____
_____
_____
_____

Equipment needed:_____
_____
_____

Project Title:_____Production Co._____

Director:_____ Page #_____

Scene:_____Shot #_____ Location:_____

```
┌─────────────────────────────────────────────────────────┐
│                                                           │
│                                                           │
│                                                           │
│                                                           │
│                                                           │
│                                                           │
│                                                           │
│                                                           │
│                                                           │
│                                                           │
│                                                           │
│                                                           │
│                                                           │
│                                                           │
│                                                           │
└─────────────────────────────────────────────────────────┘
```

Still ☐ Pan ☐ Dolly ☐ Tilt ☐ Zoom ☐ Pedestal ☐ Truck ☐ Handheld ☐

Description of action: _____

_____

_____

_____

_____

_____

_____

_____

_____

_____

Other cues: _____

_____

_____

_____

_____

Equipment needed: _____

_____

_____

_____

Project Title:_____Production Co._____

Director:_____ Page #_____

Scene:_____Shot #_____ Location:_____

Still ☐ Pan ☐ Dolly ☐ Tilt ☐ Zoom ☐ Pedestal ☐ Truck ☐ Handheld ☐

Description of action: _____

_____

_____

_____

_____

_____

_____

_____

_____

Other cues: _____

_____

_____

_____

_____

Equipment needed: _____

_____

_____

_____

Project Title:_____Production Co._____
Director:_____ Page #_____
Scene:_____Shot #_____ Location:_____

Still ☐ Pan ☐ Dolly ☐ Tilt ☐ Zoom ☐ Pedestal ☐ Truck ☐ Handheld ☐

Description of action: _____
_____
_____
_____
_____
_____
_____
_____
_____
_____
_____

Other cues: _____
_____
_____
_____
_____

Equipment needed: _____
_____
_____
_____

Project Title:_____Production Co._____

Director:_____ Page #_____

Scene:_____Shot #_____ Location:_____

```
┌─────────────────────────────────────────────────────────────────┐
│                                                                   │
│                                                                   │
│                                                                   │
│                                                                   │
│                                                                   │
│                                                                   │
│                                                                   │
│                                                                   │
│                                                                   │
│                                                                   │
│                                                                   │
│                                                                   │
│                                                                   │
│                                                                   │
│                                                                   │
└─────────────────────────────────────────────────────────────────┘
```

Still ☐ Pan ☐ Dolly ☐ Tilt ☐ Zoom ☐ Pedestal ☐ Truck ☐ Handheld ☐

Description of action: _____

_____

_____

_____

_____

_____

_____

_____

_____

Other cues: _____

_____

_____

_____

_____

Equipment needed: _____

_____

_____

_____

Project Title:_____Production Co._____

Director:_____ Page #_____

Scene:_____Shot #_____ Location:_____

Still ☐ Pan ☐ Dolly ☐ Tilt ☐ Zoom ☐ Pedestal ☐ Truck ☐ Handheld ☐

Description of action: _____

_____

_____

_____

_____

_____

_____

_____

_____

Other cues: _____

_____

_____

_____

_____

Equipment needed: _____

_____

_____

_____

Project Title:_____Production Co._____

Director:_____ Page #_____

Scene:_____Shot #_____ Location:_____

```
┌─────────────────────────────────────────────────────────┐
│                                                         │
│                                                         │
│                                                         │
│                                                         │
│                                                         │
│                                                         │
│                                                         │
│                                                         │
│                                                         │
│                                                         │
│                                                         │
│                                                         │
└─────────────────────────────────────────────────────────┘
```

Still ☐ Pan ☐ Dolly ☐ Tilt ☐ Zoom ☐ Pedestal ☐ Truck ☐ Handheld ☐

Description of action: _____

_____

_____

_____

_____

_____

_____

_____

_____

Other cues: _____

_____

_____

_____

_____

Equipment needed: _____

_____

_____

_____

Project Title:_____Production Co._____
Director:_____Page #_____
Scene:_____Shot #_____ Location:_____

```
┌─────────────────────────────────────────────────────────┐
│                                                           │
│                                                           │
│                                                           │
│                                                           │
│                                                           │
│                                                           │
│                                                           │
│                                                           │
│                                                           │
│                                                           │
│                                                           │
│                                                           │
│                                                           │
└─────────────────────────────────────────────────────────┘
```

Still ☐ Pan ☐ Dolly ☐ Tilt ☐ Zoom ☐ Pedestal ☐ Truck ☐ Handheld ☐

Description of action:_____
_____
_____
_____
_____
_____
_____
_____
_____

Other cues:_____
_____
_____
_____
_____

Equipment needed:_____
_____
_____
_____

Project Title:_____Production Co._____
Director:_____ Page #_____
Scene:_____Shot #_____ Location:_____

Still ☐ Pan ☐ Dolly ☐ Tilt ☐ Zoom ☐ Pedestal ☐ Truck ☐ Handheld ☐

Description of action: _____
_____
_____
_____
_____
_____
_____
_____
_____
_____
_____

Other cues: _____
_____
_____
_____
_____
_____

Equipment needed: _____
_____
_____
_____

Project Title:_____Production Co._____

Director:_____ Page #_____

Scene:_____Shot #_____ Location:_____

```
┌─────────────────────────────────────────────────────────┐
│                                                         │
│                                                         │
│                                                         │
│                                                         │
│                                                         │
│                                                         │
│                                                         │
│                                                         │
│                                                         │
│                                                         │
│                                                         │
│                                                         │
│                                                         │
│                                                         │
└─────────────────────────────────────────────────────────┘
```

Still ☐ Pan ☐ Dolly ☐ Tilt ☐ Zoom ☐ Pedestal ☐ Truck ☐ Handheld ☐

Description of action: _____

_____

_____

_____

_____

_____

_____

_____

_____

_____

Other cues: _____

_____

_____

_____

_____

Equipment needed: _____

_____

_____

_____

Project Title:_____Production Co._____

Director:_____ Page #_____

Scene:_____Shot #_____ Location:_____

Still ☐ Pan ☐ Dolly ☐ Tilt ☐ Zoom ☐ Pedestal ☐ Truck ☐ Handheld ☐

Description of action:_____

_____

_____

_____

_____

_____

_____

_____

_____

Other cues:_____

_____

_____

_____

_____

Equipment needed:_____

_____

_____

_____

Project Title:_____Production Co._____

Director:_____Page #_____

Scene:_____Shot #_____ Location:_____

```
┌─────────────────────────────────────────────────────────────────┐
│                                                                   │
│                                                                   │
│                                                                   │
│                                                                   │
│                                                                   │
│                                                                   │
│                                                                   │
│                                                                   │
│                                                                   │
│                                                                   │
│                                                                   │
│                                                                   │
│                                                                   │
└─────────────────────────────────────────────────────────────────┘
```

Still ☐ Pan ☐ Dolly ☐ Tilt ☐ Zoom ☐ Pedestal ☐ Truck ☐ Handheld ☐

Description of action: _____
_____
_____
_____
_____
_____
_____
_____
_____
_____

Other cues: _____
_____
_____
_____
_____

Equipment needed: _____
_____
_____
_____

Project Title:_____Production Co._____

Director:_____ Page #_____

Scene:_____ Shot #_____ Location:_____

Still ☐ Pan ☐ Dolly ☐ Tilt ☐ Zoom ☐ Pedestal ☐ Truck ☐ Handheld ☐

Description of action: _____

_____

_____

_____

_____

_____

_____

_____

_____

_____

_____

Other cues: _____

_____

_____

_____

_____

_____

Equipment needed: _____

_____

_____

_____

Project Title:_____Production Co._____

Director:_____ Page #_____

Scene:_____Shot #_____ Location:_____

Still ☐ Pan ☐ Dolly ☐ Tilt ☐ Zoom ☐ Pedestal ☐ Truck ☐ Handheld ☐

Description of action: _____

_____

_____

_____

_____

_____

_____

_____

_____

Other cues: _____

_____

_____

_____

_____

Equipment needed: _____

_____

_____

_____

Project Title:_____Production Co._____

Director:_____ Page #_____

Scene:_____Shot #_____ Location:_____

Still ☐ Pan ☐ Dolly ☐ Tilt ☐ Zoom ☐ Pedestal ☐ Truck ☐ Handheld ☐

Description of action: _____

_____

_____

_____

_____

_____

_____

_____

_____

_____

_____

Other cues: _____

_____

_____

_____

_____

Equipment needed: _____

_____

_____

_____

Project Title:_____Production Co._____

Director:_____ Page #_____

Scene:_____Shot #_____ Location:_____

Still ☐ Pan ☐ Dolly ☐ Tilt ☐ Zoom ☐ Pedestal ☐ Truck ☐ Handheld ☐

Description of action: _____

_____
_____
_____
_____
_____
_____
_____
_____
_____

Other cues: _____

_____
_____
_____
_____

Equipment needed: _____

_____
_____
_____
_____

Project Title:_____Production Co._____
Director:_____ Page #_____
Scene:_____Shot #_____ Location:_____

Still ☐ Pan ☐ Dolly ☐ Tilt ☐ Zoom ☐ Pedestal ☐ Truck ☐ Handheld ☐

Description of action: _____
_____
_____
_____
_____
_____
_____
_____
_____
_____
_____

Other cues: _____
_____
_____
_____
_____

Equipment needed: _____
_____
_____
_____
_____

Project Title:_____Production Co._____

Director:_____ Page #_____

Scene:_____Shot #_____ Location:_____

```

```

Still ☐ Pan ☐ Dolly ☐ Tilt ☐ Zoom ☐ Pedestal ☐ Truck ☐ Handheld ☐

Description of action: _____

_____

_____

_____

_____

_____

_____

_____

_____

Other cues: _____

_____

_____

_____

_____

Equipment needed: _____

_____

_____

_____

Project Title:_____Production Co._____
Director:_____ Page #_____
Scene:_____Shot #_____ Location:_____

Still ☐ Pan ☐ Dolly ☐ Tilt ☐ Zoom ☐ Pedestal ☐ Truck ☐ Handheld ☐

Description of action: _____
_____
_____
_____
_____
_____
_____
_____
_____
_____

Other cues: _____
_____
_____
_____
_____

Equipment needed: _____
_____
_____
_____

Project Title:_____Production Co._____

Director:_____ Page #_____

Scene:_____Shot #_____ Location:_____

![storyboard frame]

Still ☐ Pan ☐ Dolly ☐ Tilt ☐ Zoom ☐ Pedestal ☐ Truck ☐ Handheld ☐

Description of action: _____

_____

_____

_____

_____

_____

_____

_____

_____

_____

Other cues: _____

_____

_____

_____

_____

Equipment needed: _____

_____

_____

_____

Project Title:_____Production Co._____
Director:_____ Page #_____
Scene:_____Shot #_____ Location:_____

```

```

Still ☐ Pan ☐ Dolly ☐ Tilt ☐ Zoom ☐ Pedestal ☐ Truck ☐ Handheld ☐

Description of action: _____
_____
_____
_____
_____
_____
_____
_____
_____

Other cues: _____
_____
_____
_____
_____

Equipment needed: _____
_____
_____
_____

Project Title:_____Production Co._____
Director:_____ Page #_____
Scene:_____Shot #_____ Location:_____

[ ]

Still ☐ Pan ☐ Dolly ☐ Tilt ☐ Zoom ☐ Pedestal ☐ Truck ☐ Handheld ☐

Description of action: _____
_____
_____
_____
_____
_____
_____
_____
_____
_____

Other cues: _____
_____
_____
_____
_____

Equipment needed: _____
_____
_____
_____

Project Title:_____Production Co._____

Director:_____ Page #_____

Scene:_____Shot #_____ Location:_____

Still ☐ Pan ☐ Dolly ☐ Tilt ☐ Zoom ☐ Pedestal ☐ Truck ☐ Handheld ☐

Description of action: _____
_____
_____
_____
_____
_____
_____
_____
_____

Other cues: _____
_____
_____
_____
_____

Equipment needed: _____
_____
_____
_____

Project Title:_____Production Co._____

Director:_____ Page #_____

Scene:_____Shot #_____ Location:_____

Still ☐ Pan ☐ Dolly ☐ Tilt ☐ Zoom ☐ Pedestal ☐ Truck ☐ Handheld ☐

Description of action: _____

_____

_____

_____

_____

_____

_____

_____

_____

Other cues: _____

_____

_____

_____

_____

Equipment needed: _____

_____

_____

_____

Project Title:_____Production Co._____

Director:_____ Page #_____

Scene:_____Shot #_____ Location:_____

```
┌──────────────────────────────────────────────────────────┐
│                                                            │
│                                                            │
│                                                            │
│                                                            │
│                                                            │
│                                                            │
│                                                            │
│                                                            │
│                                                            │
│                                                            │
└──────────────────────────────────────────────────────────┘
```

Still ☐ Pan ☐ Dolly ☐ Tilt ☐ Zoom ☐ Pedestal ☐ Truck ☐ Handheld ☐

Description of action: _____

_____

_____

_____

_____

_____

_____

_____

_____

Other cues: _____

_____

_____

_____

Equipment needed: _____

_____

_____

_____

Project Title:_____Production Co._____

Director:_____ Page #_____

Scene:_____Shot #_____ Location:_____

```
┌──────────────────────────────────────────────┐
│                                                │
│                                                │
│                                                │
│                                                │
│                                                │
│                                                │
│                                                │
│                                                │
│                                                │
│                                                │
│                                                │
│                                                │
│                                                │
└──────────────────────────────────────────────┘
```

Still ☐ Pan ☐ Dolly ☐ Tilt ☐ Zoom ☐ Pedestal ☐ Truck ☐ Handheld ☐

Description of action: _____

_____

_____

_____

_____

_____

_____

_____

_____

_____

Other cues: _____

_____

_____

_____

_____

Equipment needed: _____

_____

_____

_____

Project Title:_____ Production Co._____

Director:_____ Page #_____

Scene:_____ Shot #_____ Location:_____

Still ☐ Pan ☐ Dolly ☐ Tilt ☐ Zoom ☐ Pedestal ☐ Truck ☐ Handheld ☐

Description of action: _____

_____

_____

_____

_____

_____

_____

_____

_____

Other cues: _____

_____

_____

_____

_____

Equipment needed: _____

_____

_____

_____

Project Title:_____Production Co._____

Director:_____ Page #_____

Scene:_____Shot #_____ Location:_____

```




```

Still ☐ Pan ☐ Dolly ☐ Tilt ☐ Zoom ☐ Pedestal ☐ Truck ☐ Handheld ☐

Description of action: _____

_____

_____

_____

_____

_____

_____

_____

_____

_____

Other cues: _____

_____

_____

_____

_____

Equipment needed: _____

_____

_____

_____

Project Title:_____Production Co._____

Director:_____ Page #_____

Scene:_____Shot #_____ Location:_____

```
┌─────────────────────────────────────────────────────────────┐
│                                                             │
│                                                             │
│                                                             │
│                                                             │
│                                                             │
│                                                             │
│                                                             │
│                                                             │
│                                                             │
│                                                             │
│                                                             │
│                                                             │
│                                                             │
│                                                             │
└─────────────────────────────────────────────────────────────┘
```

Still ☐ Pan ☐ Dolly ☐ Tilt ☐ Zoom ☐ Pedestal ☐ Truck ☐ Handheld ☐

Description of action: _____

_____

_____

_____

_____

_____

_____

_____

_____

_____

Other cues: _____

_____

_____

_____

_____

Equipment needed: _____

_____

_____

_____

_____

Project Title:_____Production Co._____

Director:_____ Page #_____

Scene:_____ Shot #_____ Location:_____

```



```

Still ☐ Pan ☐ Dolly ☐ Tilt ☐ Zoom ☐ Pedestal ☐ Truck ☐ Handheld ☐

Description of action:_____

_____

_____

_____

_____

_____

_____

_____

_____

_____

Other cues:_____

_____

_____

_____

_____

Equipment needed:_____

_____

_____

_____

Project Title:_____Production Co._____

Director:_____ Page #_____

Scene:_____Shot #_____ Location:_____

```
┌─────────────────────────────────────────────────────┐
│                                                     │
│                                                     │
│                                                     │
│                                                     │
│                                                     │
│                                                     │
│                                                     │
│                                                     │
│                                                     │
│                                                     │
│                                                     │
│                                                     │
└─────────────────────────────────────────────────────┘
```

Still ☐ Pan ☐ Dolly ☐ Tilt ☐ Zoom ☐ Pedestal ☐ Truck ☐ Handheld ☐

Description of action:_____

_____

_____

_____

_____

_____

_____

_____

_____

Other cues:_____

_____

_____

_____

_____

Equipment needed:_____

_____

_____

_____

Project Title:_____Production Co._____
Director:_____ Page #_____
Scene:_____Shot #_____ Location:_____

Still ☐ Pan ☐ Dolly ☐ Tilt ☐ Zoom ☐ Pedestal ☐ Truck ☐ Handheld ☐

Description of action: _____
_____
_____
_____
_____
_____
_____
_____
_____

Other cues: _____
_____
_____
_____
_____

Equipment needed: _____
_____
_____
_____

Project Title:_____ Production Co._____

Director:_____ Page #_____

Scene:_____ Shot #_____ Location:_____

```
┌─────────────────────────────────────────┐
│                                         │
│                                         │
│                                         │
│                                         │
│                                         │
│                                         │
│                                         │
│                                         │
│                                         │
│                                         │
│                                         │
│                                         │
└─────────────────────────────────────────┘
```

Still □ Pan □ Dolly □ Tilt □ Zoom □ Pedestal □ Truck □ Handheld □

Description of action: _____

_____
_____
_____
_____
_____
_____
_____
_____

Other cues: _____

_____
_____
_____
_____

Equipment needed: _____

_____
_____
_____

Project Title:_____Production Co._____

Director:_____ Page #_____

Scene:_____Shot #_____ Location:_____

```
┌──────────────────────────────────────────────┐
│                                                │
│                                                │
│                                                │
│                                                │
│                                                │
│                                                │
│                                                │
│                                                │
│                                                │
│                                                │
│                                                │
│                                                │
│                                                │
│                                                │
│                                                │
└──────────────────────────────────────────────┘
```

Still ☐ Pan ☐ Dolly ☐ Tilt ☐ Zoom ☐ Pedestal ☐ Truck ☐ Handheld ☐

Description of action: _____

_____

_____

_____

_____

_____

_____

_____

_____

_____

Other cues: _____

_____

_____

_____

_____

Equipment needed: _____

_____

_____

_____

Project Title:_____Production Co._____
Director:_____ Page #_____
Scene:_____Shot #_____ Location:_____

Still ☐ Pan ☐ Dolly ☐ Tilt ☐ Zoom ☐ Pedestal ☐ Truck ☐ Handheld ☐

Description of action: _____
_____
_____
_____
_____
_____
_____
_____
_____
_____
_____

Other cues: _____
_____
_____
_____
_____
_____

Equipment needed: _____
_____
_____
_____

Project Title:_____Production Co._____

Director:_____ Page #_____

Scene:_____Shot #_____ Location:_____

Still ☐ Pan ☐ Dolly ☐ Tilt ☐ Zoom ☐ Pedestal ☐ Truck ☐ Handheld ☐

Description of action: _____

_____

_____

_____

_____

_____

_____

_____

_____

_____

Other cues: _____

_____

_____

_____

_____

Equipment needed: _____

_____

_____

_____

Project Title:_____Production Co._____

Director:_____ Page #_____

Scene:_____Shot #_____ Location:_____

Still ☐ Pan ☐ Dolly ☐ Tilt ☐ Zoom ☐ Pedestal ☐ Truck ☐ Handheld ☐

Description of action:_____

_____

_____

_____

_____

_____

_____

_____

_____

Other cues:_____

_____

_____

_____

_____

Equipment needed:_____

_____

_____

_____

Project Title:_____Production Co._____

Director:_____ Page #_____

Scene:_____Shot #_____ Location:_____

```




```

Still ☐ Pan ☐ Dolly ☐ Tilt ☐ Zoom ☐ Pedestal ☐ Truck ☐ Handheld ☐

Description of action: _____

_____

_____

_____

_____

_____

_____

_____

Other cues: _____

_____

_____

_____

Equipment needed: _____

_____

_____

_____

Project Title:_____ Production Co._____
Director:_____ Page #_____
Scene:_____ Shot #_____ Location:_____

[ ]

Still ☐ Pan ☐ Dolly ☐ Tilt ☐ Zoom ☐ Pedestal ☐ Truck ☐ Handheld ☐

Description of action:_____
_____
_____
_____
_____
_____
_____
_____
_____
_____

Other cues:_____
_____
_____
_____
_____

Equipment needed:_____
_____
_____
_____

Project Title:_____Production Co._____

Director:_____Page #_____

Scene:_____Shot #_____ Location:_____

Still ☐ Pan ☐ Dolly ☐ Tilt ☐ Zoom ☐ Pedestal ☐ Truck ☐ Handheld ☐

Description of action: _____
_____
_____
_____
_____
_____
_____
_____
_____
_____
_____

Other cues: _____
_____
_____
_____
_____

Equipment needed: _____
_____
_____
_____

Project Title:_____Production Co._____
Director:_____ Page #_____
Scene:_____Shot #_____ Location:_____

Still ☐ Pan ☐ Dolly ☐ Tilt ☐ Zoom ☐ Pedestal ☐ Truck ☐ Handheld ☐

Description of action:_____
_____
_____
_____
_____
_____
_____
_____
_____
_____

Other cues:_____
_____
_____
_____
_____

Equipment needed:_____
_____
_____
_____

Project Title:_____Production Co._____

Director:_____ Page #_____

Scene:_____Shot #_____ Location:_____

```
┌─────────────────────────────────────────────────────────────┐
│                                                               │
│                                                               │
│                                                               │
│                                                               │
│                                                               │
│                                                               │
│                                                               │
│                                                               │
│                                                               │
│                                                               │
│                                                               │
└─────────────────────────────────────────────────────────────┘
```

Still ☐ Pan ☐ Dolly ☐ Tilt ☐ Zoom ☐ Pedestal ☐ Truck ☐ Handheld ☐

Description of action: _____

_____

_____

_____

_____

_____

_____

_____

_____

_____

Other cues: _____

_____

_____

_____

_____

Equipment needed: _____

_____

_____

_____

Project Title:_____Production Co._____
Director:_____ Page #_____
Scene:_____ Shot #_____ Location:_____

```
┌─────────────────────────────────────────────────┐
│                                                 │
│                                                 │
│                                                 │
│                                                 │
│                                                 │
│                                                 │
│                                                 │
│                                                 │
│                                                 │
│                                                 │
│                                                 │
│                                                 │
│                                                 │
│                                                 │
└─────────────────────────────────────────────────┘
```

Still ☐ Pan ☐ Dolly ☐ Tilt ☐ Zoom ☐ Pedestal ☐ Truck ☐ Handheld ☐

Description of action: _____

_____

_____

_____

_____

_____

_____

_____

_____

Other cues: _____

_____

_____

_____

Equipment needed: _____

_____

_____

_____

Project Title:_____Production Co._____
Director:_____ Page #_____
Scene:_____Shot #_____ Location:_____

```




```

Still ☐ Pan ☐ Dolly ☐ Tilt ☐ Zoom ☐ Pedestal ☐ Truck ☐ Handheld ☐

Description of action:_____
_____
_____
_____
_____
_____
_____
_____
_____

Other cues:_____
_____
_____
_____
_____

Equipment needed:_____
_____
_____
_____

Project Title:_____Production Co._____

Director:_____ Page #_____

Scene:_____ Shot #_____ Location:_____

Still ☐ Pan ☐ Dolly ☐ Tilt ☐ Zoom ☐ Pedestal ☐ Truck ☐ Handheld ☐

Description of action: _____
_____
_____
_____
_____
_____
_____
_____
_____
_____

Other cues: _____
_____
_____
_____
_____
_____

Equipment needed: _____
_____
_____
_____

Project Title:_____Production Co._____

Director:_____ Page #_____

Scene:_____Shot #_____ Location:_____

```
┌─────────────────────────────────────────────────────────┐
│                                                           │
│                                                           │
│                                                           │
│                                                           │
│                                                           │
│                                                           │
│                                                           │
│                                                           │
│                                                           │
│                                                           │
│                                                           │
│                                                           │
│                                                           │
└─────────────────────────────────────────────────────────┘
```

Still ☐ Pan ☐ Dolly ☐ Tilt ☐ Zoom ☐ Pedestal ☐ Truck ☐ Handheld ☐

Description of action: _____

_____

_____

_____

_____

_____

_____

_____

_____

Other cues: _____

_____

_____

_____

_____

Equipment needed: _____

_____

_____

_____

Project Title:_____Production Co._____
Director:_____ Page #_____
Scene:_____Shot #_____ Location:_____

```
┌─────────────────────────────────────────────────────────┐
│                                                         │
│                                                         │
│                                                         │
│                                                         │
│                                                         │
│                                                         │
│                                                         │
│                                                         │
│                                                         │
│                                                         │
│                                                         │
│                                                         │
└─────────────────────────────────────────────────────────┘
```

Still ☐ Pan ☐ Dolly ☐ Tilt ☐ Zoom ☐ Pedestal ☐ Truck ☐ Handheld ☐

Description of action: _____
_____
_____
_____
_____
_____
_____
_____
_____

Other cues: _____
_____
_____
_____
_____

Equipment needed: _____
_____
_____
_____

Project Title:_____Production Co._____
Director:_____ Page #_____
Scene:_____Shot #_____ Location:_____

Still ☐ Pan ☐ Dolly ☐ Tilt ☐ Zoom ☐ Pedestal ☐ Truck ☐ Handheld ☐

Description of action:_____
_____
_____
_____
_____
_____
_____
_____
_____
_____
_____

Other cues:_____
_____
_____
_____
_____

Equipment needed:_____
_____
_____
_____

Project Title:_____Production Co._____

Director:_____ Page #_____

Scene:_____Shot #_____ Location:_____

[ ]

Still ☐ Pan ☐ Dolly ☐ Tilt ☐ Zoom ☐ Pedestal ☐ Truck ☐ Handheld ☐

Description of action: _____
_____
_____
_____
_____
_____
_____
_____
_____
_____

Other cues: _____
_____
_____
_____
_____

Equipment needed: _____
_____
_____
_____

Project Title:_____Production Co._____

Director:_____ Page #_____

Scene:_____Shot #_____ Location:_____

Still ☐ Pan ☐ Dolly ☐ Tilt ☐ Zoom ☐ Pedestal ☐ Truck ☐ Handheld ☐

Description of action: _____

_____

_____

_____

_____

_____

_____

_____

_____

Other cues: _____

_____

_____

_____

_____

Equipment needed: _____

_____

_____

_____

Project Title:_____Production Co._____

Director:_____ Page #_____

Scene:_____Shot #_____ Location:_____

Still ☐ Pan ☐ Dolly ☐ Tilt ☐ Zoom ☐ Pedestal ☐ Truck ☐ Handheld ☐

Description of action: _____

_____

_____

_____

_____

_____

_____

_____

_____

Other cues: _____

_____

_____

_____

_____

Equipment needed: _____

_____

_____

_____

Project Title:_____Production Co._____

Director:_____ Page #_____

Scene:_____Shot #_____ Location:_____

```




```

Still ☐ Pan ☐ Dolly ☐ Tilt ☐ Zoom ☐ Pedestal ☐ Truck ☐ Handheld ☐

Description of action: _____

_____

_____

_____

_____

_____

_____

_____

_____

Other cues: _____

_____

_____

_____

Equipment needed: _____

_____

_____

_____

Project Title:_____Production Co._____

Director:_____ Page #_____

Scene:_____Shot #_____ Location:_____

Still ☐ Pan ☐ Dolly ☐ Tilt ☐ Zoom ☐ Pedestal ☐ Truck ☐ Handheld ☐

Description of action: _____

_____
_____
_____
_____
_____
_____
_____
_____
_____

Other cues: _____

_____
_____
_____
_____

Equipment needed: _____

_____
_____
_____

Project Title:_____ Production Co._____

Director:_____ Page #_____

Scene:_____ Shot #_____ Location:_____

```




```

Still ☐ Pan ☐ Dolly ☐ Tilt ☐ Zoom ☐ Pedestal ☐ Truck ☐ Handheld ☐

Description of action: _____

_____

_____

_____

_____

_____

_____

_____

_____

_____

Other cues: _____

_____

_____

_____

_____

Equipment needed: _____

_____

_____

_____

Project Title:_____Production Co._____

Director:_____ Page #_____

Scene:_____Shot #_____ Location:_____

```
┌──────────────────────────────────────────────┐
│                                              │
│                                              │
│                                              │
│                                              │
│                                              │
│                                              │
│                                              │
│                                              │
│                                              │
│                                              │
│                                              │
│                                              │
│                                              │
│                                              │
└──────────────────────────────────────────────┘
```

Still ☐ Pan ☐ Dolly ☐ Tilt ☐ Zoom ☐ Pedestal ☐ Truck ☐ Handheld ☐

Description of action: _____

_____

_____

_____

_____

_____

_____

_____

_____

Other cues: _____

_____

_____

_____

_____

Equipment needed: _____

_____

_____

_____

Project Title:_____Production Co._____

Director:_____ Page #_____

Scene:_____Shot #_____ Location:_____

Still □ Pan □ Dolly □ Tilt □ Zoom □ Pedestal □ Truck □ Handheld □

Description of action: _____

_____

_____

_____

_____

_____

_____

_____

_____

Other cues: _____

_____

_____

_____

_____

Equipment needed: _____

_____

_____

_____

Project Title:_____Production Co._____
Director:_____ Page #_____
Scene:_____ Shot #_____ Location:_____

Still ☐ Pan ☐ Dolly ☐ Tilt ☐ Zoom ☐ Pedestal ☐ Truck ☐ Handheld ☐

Description of action: _____
_____
_____
_____
_____
_____
_____
_____
_____
_____
_____

Other cues: _____
_____
_____
_____
_____

Equipment needed: _____
_____
_____
_____

Project Title:_____Production Co._____

Director:_____ Page #_____

Scene:_____Shot #_____ Location:_____

Still ☐ Pan ☐ Dolly ☐ Tilt ☐ Zoom ☐ Pedestal ☐ Truck ☐ Handheld ☐

Description of action: _____

_____

_____

_____

_____

_____

_____

_____

_____

Other cues: _____

_____

_____

_____

_____

Equipment needed: _____

_____

_____

_____

Project Title:_____Production Co._____

Director:_____ Page #_____

Scene:_____ Shot #_____ Location:_____

Still ☐ Pan ☐ Dolly ☐ Tilt ☐ Zoom ☐ Pedestal ☐ Truck ☐ Handheld ☐

Description of action: _____

_____

_____

_____

_____

_____

_____

_____

_____

Other cues: _____

_____

_____

_____

_____

Equipment needed: _____

_____

_____

_____

Project Title:_____Production Co._____

Director:_____ Page #_____

Scene:_____Shot #_____ Location:_____

```
┌─────────────────────────────────────────────────────┐
│                                                     │
│                                                     │
│                                                     │
│                                                     │
│                                                     │
│                                                     │
│                                                     │
│                                                     │
│                                                     │
│                                                     │
│                                                     │
└─────────────────────────────────────────────────────┘
```

Still ☐ Pan ☐ Dolly ☐ Tilt ☐ Zoom ☐ Pedestal ☐ Truck ☐ Handheld ☐

Description of action: _____

_____

_____

_____

_____

_____

_____

_____

_____

Other cues: _____

_____

_____

_____

_____

Equipment needed: _____

_____

_____

_____

Project Title:_____Production Co._____

Director:_____ Page #_____

Scene:_____Shot #_____ Location:_____

```
┌──────────────────────────────────────────────────┐
│                                                    │
│                                                    │
│                                                    │
│                                                    │
│                                                    │
│                                                    │
│                                                    │
│                                                    │
│                                                    │
│                                                    │
│                                                    │
└──────────────────────────────────────────────────┘
```

Still ☐ Pan ☐ Dolly ☐ Tilt ☐ Zoom ☐ Pedestal ☐ Truck ☐ Handheld ☐

Description of action: _____

_____

_____

_____

_____

_____

_____

_____

_____

Other cues: _____

_____

_____

_____

_____

Equipment needed: _____

_____

_____

_____

Project Title:_____Production Co._____

Director:_____ Page #_____

Scene:_____Shot #_____ Location:_____

Still ☐ Pan ☐ Dolly ☐ Tilt ☐ Zoom ☐ Pedestal ☐ Truck ☐ Handheld ☐

Description of action: _____

_____

_____

_____

_____

_____

_____

_____

_____

Other cues: _____

_____

_____

_____

_____

Equipment needed: _____

_____

_____

Project Title:_____Production Co._____
Director:_____ Page #_____
Scene:_____Shot #_____ Location:_____

```
┌─────────────────────────────────────────────────────────┐
│                                                         │
│                                                         │
│                                                         │
│                                                         │
│                                                         │
│                                                         │
│                                                         │
│                                                         │
│                                                         │
│                                                         │
│                                                         │
│                                                         │
│                                                         │
│                                                         │
└─────────────────────────────────────────────────────────┘
```

Still ☐ Pan ☐ Dolly ☐ Tilt ☐ Zoom ☐ Pedestal ☐ Truck ☐ Handheld ☐

Description of action: _____
_____
_____
_____
_____
_____
_____
_____
_____
_____
_____

Other cues: _____
_____
_____
_____
_____

Equipment needed: _____
_____
_____
_____

Project Title:_____Production Co._____

Director:_____ Page #_____

Scene:_____Shot #_____ Location:_____

```
┌─────────────────────────────────────────────────────┐
│                                                       │
│                                                       │
│                                                       │
│                                                       │
│                                                       │
│                                                       │
│                                                       │
│                                                       │
│                                                       │
│                                                       │
│                                                       │
│                                                       │
│                                                       │
└─────────────────────────────────────────────────────┘
```

Still □ Pan □ Dolly □ Tilt □ Zoom □ Pedestal □ Truck □ Handheld □

Description of action: _____

_____

_____

_____

_____

_____

_____

_____

_____

_____

Other cues: _____

_____

_____

_____

_____

Equipment needed: _____

_____

_____

_____

Project Title:_____Production Co._____

Director:_____ Page #_____

Scene:_____Shot #_____ Location:_____

Still ☐ Pan ☐ Dolly ☐ Tilt ☐ Zoom ☐ Pedestal ☐ Truck ☐ Handheld ☐

Description of action: _____

_____
_____
_____
_____
_____
_____
_____
_____
_____

Other cues: _____

_____
_____
_____
_____

Equipment needed: _____

_____
_____
_____

Project Title:_____Production Co._____
Director:_____ Page #_____
Scene:_____Shot #_____ Location:_____

Still ☐ Pan ☐ Dolly ☐ Tilt ☐ Zoom ☐ Pedestal ☐ Truck ☐ Handheld ☐

Description of action: _____
_____
_____
_____
_____
_____
_____
_____
_____
_____

Other cues: _____
_____
_____
_____
_____

Equipment needed: _____
_____
_____
_____

Project Title:_____Production Co._____

Director:_____ Page #_____

Scene:_____Shot #_____ Location:_____

Still ☐ Pan ☐ Dolly ☐ Tilt ☐ Zoom ☐ Pedestal ☐ Truck ☐ Handheld ☐

Description of action:_____
_____
_____
_____
_____
_____
_____
_____
_____

Other cues:_____
_____
_____
_____
_____

Equipment needed:_____
_____
_____
_____

Project Title:_____Production Co._____
Director:_____ Page #_____
Scene:_____Shot #_____ Location:_____

[shot box — empty]

Still ☐ Pan ☐ Dolly ☐ Tilt ☐ Zoom ☐ Pedestal ☐ Truck ☐ Handheld ☐

Description of action: _____
_____
_____
_____
_____
_____
_____
_____
_____
_____

Other cues: _____
_____
_____
_____
_____

Equipment needed: _____
_____
_____
_____

Project Title:_____Production Co._____

Director:_____ Page #_____

Scene:_____Shot #_____ Location:_____

```
┌─────────────────────────────────────────────────────────────────┐
│                                                                   │
│                                                                   │
│                                                                   │
│                                                                   │
│                                                                   │
│                                                                   │
│                                                                   │
│                                                                   │
│                                                                   │
│                                                                   │
│                                                                   │
│                                                                   │
│                                                                   │
│                                                                   │
└─────────────────────────────────────────────────────────────────┘
```

Still ☐ Pan ☐ Dolly ☐ Tilt ☐ Zoom ☐ Pedestal ☐ Truck ☐ Handheld ☐

Description of action: _____

_____

_____

_____

_____

_____

_____

_____

_____

_____

Other cues: _____

_____

_____

_____

_____

Equipment needed: _____

_____

_____

_____

Project Title:_____Production Co._____

Director:_____ Page #_____

Scene:_____ Shot #_____ Location:_____

```
┌─────────────────────────────────────────────────────────────┐
│                                                             │
│                                                             │
│                                                             │
│                                                             │
│                                                             │
│                                                             │
│                                                             │
│                                                             │
│                                                             │
│                                                             │
│                                                             │
│                                                             │
│                                                             │
│                                                             │
└─────────────────────────────────────────────────────────────┘
```

Still ☐ Pan ☐ Dolly ☐ Tilt ☐ Zoom ☐ Pedestal ☐ Truck ☐ Handheld ☐

Description of action:_____

_____
_____
_____
_____
_____
_____
_____
_____
_____

Other cues:_____

_____
_____
_____
_____

Equipment needed:_____

_____
_____
_____

Project Title:_____Production Co._____
Director:_____ Page #_____
Scene:_____Shot #_____ Location:_____

```



```

Still ☐ Pan ☐ Dolly ☐ Tilt ☐ Zoom ☐ Pedestal ☐ Truck ☐ Handheld ☐

Description of action: _____
_____
_____
_____
_____
_____
_____
_____
_____
_____

Other cues: _____
_____
_____
_____
_____

Equipment needed: _____
_____
_____
_____
_____

Project Title:_____Production Co._____

Director:_____ Page #_____

Scene:_____Shot #_____ Location:_____

┌───┐
│   │
│   │
│   │
│   │
│   │
│   │
│   │
│   │
│   │
│   │
│   │
│   │
│   │
│   │
└───┘

Still ☐ Pan ☐ Dolly ☐ Tilt ☐ Zoom ☐ Pedestal ☐ Truck ☐ Handheld ☐

Description of action: _____

_____

_____

_____

_____

_____

_____

_____

_____

Other cues: _____

_____

_____

_____

Equipment needed: _____

_____

_____

_____

Project Title:_____Production Co._____
Director:_____ Page #_____
Scene:_____Shot #_____ Location:_____

```
┌─────────────────────────────────────────────────────┐
│                                                     │
│                                                     │
│                                                     │
│                                                     │
│                                                     │
│                                                     │
│                                                     │
│                                                     │
│                                                     │
│                                                     │
│                                                     │
│                                                     │
│                                                     │
│                                                     │
└─────────────────────────────────────────────────────┘
```

Still □ Pan □ Dolly □ Tilt □ Zoom □ Pedestal □ Truck □ Handheld □

Description of action: _____
_____
_____
_____
_____
_____
_____
_____
_____
_____

Other cues: _____
_____
_____
_____
_____

Equipment needed: _____
_____
_____
_____

Project Title:_____Production Co._____
Director:_____ Page #_____
Scene:_____ Shot #_____ Location:_____

```
┌─────────────────────────────────────────────────────────┐
│                                                         │
│                                                         │
│                                                         │
│                                                         │
│                                                         │
│                                                         │
│                                                         │
│                                                         │
│                                                         │
│                                                         │
│                                                         │
│                                                         │
└─────────────────────────────────────────────────────────┘
```

Still ☐ Pan ☐ Dolly ☐ Tilt ☐ Zoom ☐ Pedestal ☐ Truck ☐ Handheld ☐

Description of action: _____
_____
_____
_____
_____
_____
_____
_____
_____
_____

Other cues: _____
_____
_____
_____
_____

Equipment needed: _____
_____
_____
_____

Project Title:_____Production Co._____
Director:_____ Page #_____
Scene:_____Shot #_____ Location:_____

[ ]

Still ☐ Pan ☐ Dolly ☐ Tilt ☐ Zoom ☐ Pedestal ☐ Truck ☐ Handheld ☐

Description of action: _____
_____
_____
_____
_____
_____
_____
_____
_____
_____

Other cues: _____
_____
_____
_____
_____

Equipment needed: _____
_____
_____
_____

Project Title:_____Production Co._____

Director:_____ Page #_____

Scene:_____Shot #_____ Location:_____

```
┌─────────────────────────────────────────────────────┐
│                                                       │
│                                                       │
│                                                       │
│                                                       │
│                                                       │
│                                                       │
│                                                       │
│                                                       │
│                                                       │
│                                                       │
│                                                       │
│                                                       │
│                                                       │
│                                                       │
│                                                       │
│                                                       │
└─────────────────────────────────────────────────────┘
```

Still ☐ Pan ☐ Dolly ☐ Tilt ☐ Zoom ☐ Pedestal ☐ Truck ☐ Handheld ☐

Description of action:_____

_____

_____

_____

_____

_____

_____

_____

_____

_____

Other cues:_____

_____

_____

_____

_____

Equipment needed:_____

_____

_____

_____

Project Title:_____Production Co._____

Director:_____ Page #_____

Scene:_____Shot #_____ Location:_____

```
┌─────────────────────────────────────────────────────────────┐
│                                                             │
│                                                             │
│                                                             │
│                                                             │
│                                                             │
│                                                             │
│                                                             │
│                                                             │
│                                                             │
│                                                             │
│                                                             │
│                                                             │
└─────────────────────────────────────────────────────────────┘
```

Still ☐ Pan ☐ Dolly ☐ Tilt ☐ Zoom ☐ Pedestal ☐ Truck ☐ Handheld ☐

Description of action: _____
_____
_____
_____
_____
_____
_____
_____
_____
_____

Other cues: _____
_____
_____
_____
_____

Equipment needed: _____
_____
_____
_____

Project Title:_____Production Co._____
Director:_____ Page #_____
Scene:_____Shot #_____ Location:_____

```
┌─────────────────────────────────────────────────┐
│                                                 │
│                                                 │
│                                                 │
│                                                 │
│                                                 │
│                                                 │
│                                                 │
│                                                 │
│                                                 │
│                                                 │
│                                                 │
│                                                 │
│                                                 │
│                                                 │
└─────────────────────────────────────────────────┘
```

Still ☐ Pan ☐ Dolly ☐ Tilt ☐ Zoom ☐ Pedestal ☐ Truck ☐ Handheld ☐

Description of action: _____

_____

_____

_____

_____

_____

_____

_____

_____

Other cues: _____

_____

_____

_____

_____

Equipment needed: _____

_____

_____

_____

Project Title:_____Production Co._____

Director:_____ Page #_____

Scene:_____Shot #_____ Location:_____

```
┌─────────────────────────────────────────────────────────┐
│                                                         │
│                                                         │
│                                                         │
│                                                         │
│                                                         │
│                                                         │
│                                                         │
│                                                         │
│                                                         │
│                                                         │
│                                                         │
│                                                         │
│                                                         │
│                                                         │
│                                                         │
└─────────────────────────────────────────────────────────┘
```

Still □ Pan □ Dolly □ Tilt □ Zoom □ Pedestal □ Truck □ Handheld □

Description of action: _____

_____

_____

_____

_____

_____

_____

_____

_____

_____

Other cues: _____

_____

_____

_____

_____

Equipment needed: _____

_____

_____

_____

Project Title:_____Production Co._____

Director:_____ Page #_____

Scene:_____Shot #_____ Location:_____

Still ☐ Pan ☐ Dolly ☐ Tilt ☐ Zoom ☐ Pedestal ☐ Truck ☐ Handheld ☐

Description of action: _____

_____

_____

_____

_____

_____

_____

_____

_____

Other cues: _____

_____

_____

_____

_____

Equipment needed: _____

_____

_____

_____

_____

Project Title:_____Production Co._____

Director:_____ Page #_____

Scene:_____Shot #_____ Location:_____

```
┌─────────────────────────────────────────────────────────┐
│                                                         │
│                                                         │
│                                                         │
│                                                         │
│                                                         │
│                                                         │
│                                                         │
│                                                         │
│                                                         │
│                                                         │
│                                                         │
│                                                         │
│                                                         │
│                                                         │
│                                                         │
│                                                         │
└─────────────────────────────────────────────────────────┘
```

Still ☐ Pan ☐ Dolly ☐ Tilt ☐ Zoom ☐ Pedestal ☐ Truck ☐ Handheld ☐

Description of action: _____

_____
_____
_____
_____
_____
_____
_____
_____
_____

Other cues: _____

_____
_____
_____
_____
_____

Equipment needed: _____

_____
_____
_____

Project Title:_____Production Co._____

Director:_____ Page #_____

Scene:_____Shot #_____ Location:_____

```
┌─────────────────────────────────────────────────────────────┐
│                                                             │
│                                                             │
│                                                             │
│                                                             │
│                                                             │
│                                                             │
│                                                             │
│                                                             │
│                                                             │
│                                                             │
│                                                             │
│                                                             │
│                                                             │
│                                                             │
└─────────────────────────────────────────────────────────────┘
```

Still ☐ Pan ☐ Dolly ☐ Tilt ☐ Zoom ☐ Pedestal ☐ Truck ☐ Handheld ☐

Description of action: _____

_____

_____

_____

_____

_____

_____

_____

_____

Other cues: _____

_____

_____

_____

_____

Equipment needed: _____

_____

_____

_____

www.ingramcontent.com/pod-product-compliance
Lightning Source LLC
Chambersburg PA
CBHW080421290526
45791CB00008BA/2368